Published in 2019 by The Rosen Publishing Group, Inc.
29 East 21st Street, New York, NY 10010

First Edition

Library of Congress Cataloging-in-Publication Data

Names: Mayer, Melissa, author.
Title: Coping with date rape and acquaintance rape / Melissa Mayer.
Description: New York : Rosen Publishing, 2019 | Series: Coping | Audience: Grades 7–12. | Includes bibliographical references and index.
Identifiers: LCCN 2018011714| ISBN 9781508183167 (library bound) | ISBN 9781508183150 (pbk.)
Subjects: LCSH: Date rape—Juvenile literature. | Sex crimes—Juvenile literature.
Classification: LCC HQ801.83 .M395 2019 | DDC 362.883—dc23
LC record available at https://lccn.loc.gov/2018011714

Manufactured in China

CONTENTS

INTRODUCTION...4

CHAPTER ONE
What Are Date Rape and Acquaintance Rape?................7

CHAPTER TWO
Types of Date Rape and Acquaintance Rape.................22

CHAPTER THREE
The Effects of Sexual Violence..................................36

CHAPTER FOUR
Understanding Rape Culture.....................................51

CHAPTER FIVE
What to Do if You Are Raped.....................................66

CHAPTER SIX
Responding to Sexual Violence
and Rape Culture...78

GLOSSARY   95
FOR MORE INFORMATION   98
FOR FURTHER READING   103
BIBLIOGRAPHY   105
INDEX   108

INTRODUCTION

Few topics are as harrowing as sexual violence. In part, this is because rape is more than just run-of-the-mill violence; it is an assault on the most vulnerable, intimate self. It is also difficult to read and talk about because the statistics are so bleak; a shocking percentage of people, especially girls and women, will experience sexual assault firsthand. Certainly, over the course of a lifetime, everyone will know someone who is a survivor of sexual violence.

And yet the ubiquitous nature of sexual violence is why it is so important to read, write, and talk openly about it. At its very core, rape is not a crime centered around sexuality or desire but rather a criminal act related to power. When you experience rape—or perhaps even when you read or think about sexual violence—it can feel as if your authority over your own body, your agency, has been stolen, leaving you powerless.

Sexual violence holds power over people because of its ability to make survivors feel small and silenced. But strength comes in numbers, and many voices rising together can shatter the code of silence surrounding sexual assault and rape. By talking honestly and bravely about experiences of sexual violence and the culture that makes it possible, people can begin to name and understand rape, sexual assault, and other forms of sexual violence that are often ignored or minimized.

Reading or talking about sexual violence can feel distressing, but confronting sexual abuse and rape head-on may help you reclaim your power.

This is especially important when confronting sexual violence that occurs at the hands of someone you know, trust, and maybe even love. Date rape and acquaintance rape are particularly destructive because of the way they violate not only your body but also the belief that you can trust your judgment and the people closest to you. These acts can shake both your physical and emotional safety.

Learning about sexual violence serves two functions. One is to help you gain a better understanding of date rape and acquaintance rape and know what to do if you (or someone you care about) experience sexual violence firsthand. The other is an invitation to think about how outdated ideas about gender and sexuality create an environment in which date rape and acquaintance rape seem normal or even expected, creating barriers for survivors seeking justice and healing.

When talking about people who have experienced sexual violence, it is appropriate to choose empowering language, such as replacing the word "victim" with "survivor." This is because sexual violence is about taking away someone's power. Framing the discourse about rape and people who experience rape is one way to return that power where it belongs. If you have experienced sexual violence, you did not have a choice about being the victim of that crime—nothing you did or didn't do caused it to happen—but you do decide every day to survive those circumstances. And that is a powerful choice.

What Are Date Rape and Acquaintance Rape?

CHAPTER ONE

Perhaps because sexual violence is so shocking and intimate, it is often used as a storyline in popular culture and media. Rape is such a common entertainment trope that entire series are written describing the imagined drama of investigating and prosecuting rape, and it's hard to read the news without also reading about sexual violence. In part, this is because the notion of rape taps into fears, and that draws people's attention, but it is also because sexual violence is familiar and therefore makes for plausible, relatable content. This illustrates how sexual violence is an embedded part of the cultural experience—and how easy it is to focus on the shock of the crime itself and leave out recovery, prevention, and education.

To extract the truth about sexual violence, it is necessary to get down to the bare bones of the issue: how often rape occurs and what it actually looks like.

How Common Is Rape?

According to the Rape, Abuse, and Incest National Network (RAINN), the statistics associated with sexual violence are pretty grim. RAINN reports that a sexual assault occurs in the United States every ninety-eight seconds and that one out of every six women (and one out of every thirty-three men) will experience rape or attempted rape in their lifetimes. When most people think about rape, they imagine stranger rape, but that is actually the least common type of sexual violence. Shockingly, the bulk of sexual violence (70 percent) is perpetrated by someone the survivor knows. This is known as acquaintance rape.

According to the statistics, acquaintance rape is particularly

"Me Too" was first coined by civil rights activist Tarana Burke in 2006 to highlight the pervasive nature of sexual violence. The phrase went viral as a hashtag in 2017.

common for young adults. RAINN indicates that women who are sixteen to nineteen years old are four times more likely to experience sexual violence compared with the general population. Of the children and teens whose sexual abuse cases are reported to law enforcement, almost all of them (93 percent) were perpetrated by acquaintances or family members.

In addition to young people, people of color (especially indigenous women, who are twice as likely to be raped as all other people), members of the LGBTQIA community, and people with disabilities are all more vulnerable to sexual violence. For people with a number of these identities, that risk is compounded.

The statistics aren't all terrible. RAINN reports that the overall rate of rape and sexual assault fell by 63 percent between 1993 and 2014. Even so, for the individuals who experience rape, the repercussions can be life altering. Approximately 70 percent of survivors of sexual

Anyone can experience sexual violence. But young women, people of color, the LGBTQIA community, and people with disabilities are the most vulnerable to this type of violence.

violence report moderate to severe distress—much higher than any other violent crime. Almost all women who experience rape (94 percent) experience post-traumatic stress disorder (PTSD) symptoms immediately following the rape, and one-third even consider suicide.

What Exactly Is Rape?

Because rape is a crime generally prosecuted at the state level, the definitions that govern what precise acts meet the legal standard for rape or other sex crimes can vary from state to state. The most straightforward definition of rape is the federal definition, written by the FBI. It describes rape as "penetration, no matter how slight, of the vagina or anus with any body part or object, or oral penetration by a sex organ of another person,

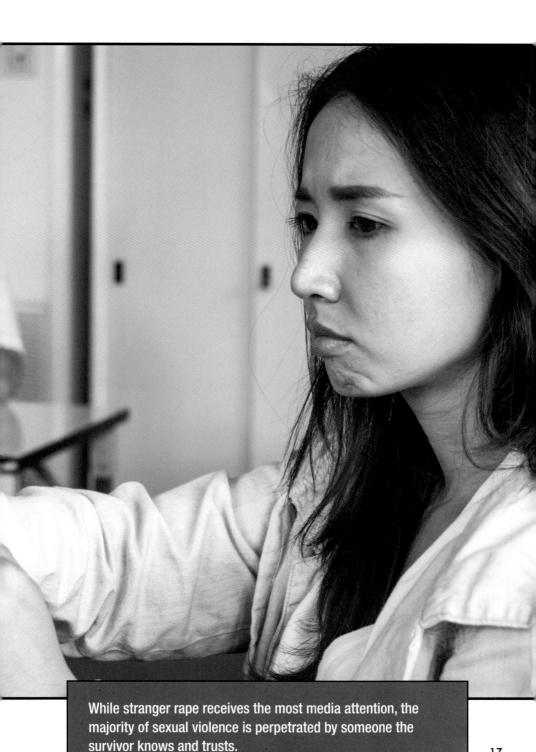

While stranger rape receives the most media attention, the majority of sexual violence is perpetrated by someone the survivor knows and trusts.

without the consent of the victim." It is important to note that this is much more specific than the term "sexual assault," which includes any sexual contact done without explicit consent from all parties.

When most people imagine rape, they think of craven strangers lurking in the shadows as they walk home in the dark or unknown assailants selecting their victims by chance. Most people probably only picture forcible heterosexual intercourse and only "count" rape that is completed. But this is inaccurate. Most of the time, rapists are people their victims know, and rape (and certainly sexual assault) can take many forms. Furthermore, an attempted rape is still a rape. This is important because the messages you receive about what rape looks like can stick in your mind and leave you uncertain or confused if you experience something you know to be wrong but that differs from what you imagined.

Depending on how the survivor and perpetrator know each other, experts sometimes use specific terminology for describing rape. For instance, the most general term for rape perpetrated by someone the survivor knows is acquaintance rape. When rape is perpetrated by a romantic partner or someone the survivor is dating (or to whom she is married), this is date rape (or marital rape).

Examples of Consent and Nonconsent

Consent Is:
- Checking in when you change activities or intensity: "Is this OK?"
- Speaking up or using your body to convey that you agree to the activity.
- Talking about activities before you try them.
- Viewing sex as a mutual activity and not an individual entitlement.
- Respecting your partner's feelings, beliefs, and preferences, even if they differ from your own.
- Considering your partner's needs and desires to be equal to your own.

Consent Is Not:
- Assuming something is OK because you have done it before.
- Assuming someone will be physical with you because they have had sex with someone else.
- Ignoring "no" or negative body language from your partner.
- Believing that paying for dates or giving gifts means that someone owes you sex.

(continued on the next page)

(continued from the previous page)

- Assuming the way someone dresses or acts (for example, flirting) means that he or she will agree to sexual activity.
- Assuming that kissing or engaging in one sexual activity means that your partner agrees to more.
- Pressuring someone with fear or intimidation.
- Continuing to ask someone to do something after he or she has said no or told you to stop.
- Sulking or emotionally manipulating your partner into changing his mind.
- Taking advantage of someone who has been using drugs or alcohol or who is too young to legally consent.

What Is Consent?

When it comes to rape and sexual assault, the most important word to define and understand is a powerful one: consent. You already know that sexual violence is some form of sexual activity that happens without consent—but what, exactly, does consent look like?

The general definition of consent is permission or agreement for something to happen. When it comes to sex, the agreements you make and permissions you give aren't always a simple yes or no. It is this room for ambiguity that makes it possible for some people to write off nonconsensual experiences as "just bad sex"

You always have the right to give or withhold your consent in any sexual situation. Respecting your partners' consent shows that you care about them.

17

or to minimize sexual violence as a misunderstanding. Changing the statistics associated with rape requires getting serious about understanding and respecting consent all the time.

Experts often describe sexual consent as explicit or enthusiastic, but there are actually several facets of consent that can help you recognize consensual sex and make it the standard you expect with your partners. According to Planned Parenthood, consent should be ongoing, freely given, specific, informed, and enthusiastic. It's important to look at each of those characteristics one at a time.

Ongoing consent means that you can change your mind at any time. If, for any reason, you decide that you want to stop having sex after you have already started, you have the right to change your mind. There is not a point of no return with sex; stopping is always an option.

Freely given consent means that you made the agreement without any pressure or manipulation. If someone tries to intimidate you or persuade you to do something you aren't sure about, your consent is not freely given. If you say yes because you are afraid to say no, that is not freely given consent.

Specific consent means that if you give permission for one thing, your partner should not assume that you have agreed to anything more. For instance, if you agree to kiss someone or have oral sex, your partner should not assume that this means you also give permission for intercourse.

Informed consent means that you understand what you are agreeing to and that no one deceived you or lied to you. If you are intoxicated, your consent can't be informed. Another example is nonconsensual condom removal (stealthing). If two people agree to sex with a condom but one partner slips the condom off without the other person's knowledge or agreement, this is deceit and it violates consent.

Enthusiastic consent means that you agree to do something because you want to do it and not because you feel obligated to do it. Sex is not an entitlement; you never owe anyone access to your body.

Sometimes people learn about consent and find it overwhelming. They throw their hands up and say that it will be too difficult to ever figure out if someone is agreeing to consensual sex. Or they worry that setting expectations for clear consent will somehow strip the romance from sexual relationships. This isn't true. Consent is really just a detailed way of saying that sexual partners should respect each other and treat each other with consideration. The truth is that romance and healthy sexuality can't exist unless they include mutual respect.

Myths & FACTS

Myth: If you dress or act a certain way, you are asking to be raped.

Fact: Nobody asks to be raped, and nothing you wear or do could make rape your fault. Judging someone's style of dress or behavior as "asking for it" is called slut shaming and is never OK. It's important to remember that rape is always the perpetrator's fault; the survivor is never to blame.

Myth: It isn't rape if you've been intimate before.

Fact: Every single time that you are intimate with someone, you have the option to give your consent—or not to give it. Having a previous sexual relationship (with your current partner or someone else) has nothing to do with consent in the present moment. You don't owe anyone access to your body. You can even change your mind in the middle of being intimate with someone.

Myth: Rape happens only to women.

Fact: While most rape survivors are women, 10 percent of rape survivors are men. On top of being inaccurate, this myth makes it more difficult for boys and men to seek help after having been raped. Current reporting makes it difficult to cite statistics for survivors who identify as agender, genderqueer, or nonbinary.

Myth: If it was really rape, you would fight back.

Fact: Your reaction to being raped has no bearing on the definition of rape. Some people respond to adrenaline by fighting or fleeing, and some people respond by freezing. All three responses are valid. Even if you don't fight back, it is still rape.

CHAPTER TWO

Types of Date Rape and Acquaintance Rape

The myths and misunderstandings surrounding acquaintance rape persist in large part because it can be uncomfortable to talk openly about rape—especially rape perpetrated by someone you know. The truth is that sexual violence is not just one very specific, very distant act but rather a cluster of related crimes. This means that the sexual violence one person experiences can look different from what another person experiences, and perhaps neither one resembles the imagined standard of stranger rape. To address this, it's a good idea to develop a broad understanding of some of the more common types of acquaintance rape.

Partner Rape or Marital Rape

All forms of acquaintance rape were once called "date rape," with the incorrect assumption that sexual violence was generally perpetrated by either a stranger or a date. For this reason, partner rape or marital rape might be the most recognizable form of acquaintance rape. While it includes rape that happens on a date,

Sexual violence can happen inside a relationship or marriage. Just because you are married to someone, that doesn't mean you owe that person access to your body.

23

of course, partner rape is really any rape in which the perpetrator and survivor are romantically involved. This could be a blind date, a boyfriend or girlfriend, a domestic partner, or even a spouse. Statistics for partner rape usually include ex-partners as well, since the primary connection between the perpetrator and survivor is a romantic one.

According to RAINN, 25 percent of rapes are perpetrated by a current or former partner. It is sometimes surprising for people to learn that rape can happen in the context of a marriage, but it reveals something even more startling: marital rape has only been illegal in all fifty US states since 1993. Before that, some states maintained provisions excusing rape that happened between spouses as somehow different from other sexual violence.

Even though the United Nations has defined marital rape as a human rights violation, it remains accepted in some parts of the world. This notion is based on the false idea that spouses (especially women) give up their sexual agency when they take marriage vows and that consent is now always implied because the partners owe each other unrestricted access to their bodies. This is not true; even within the context of marriage, sexual activity requires your consent. It is important to know that even if you are in a relationship or have had sex with someone before, any sex without your consent is rape.

Acquaintance Rape

By far the most common category of rape is general acquaintance rape. According to RAINN, acquaintance rape accounts for 45 percent of all rapes. An acquaintance is someone the survivor knows in any context. This includes employers or coworkers, neighbors, friends, fellow students, and even people in positions of authority, like teachers, doctors, or religious leaders. It also includes family members (1 percent of all rapes), although rape perpetrated by a family member is specifically called incest.

While it is relatively easy to search for information about stranger rape or date rape, the broader category of acquaintance rape yields fewer results. This says a lot about the conversations society is avoiding about sexual violence, and it also explains why some researchers call acquaintance rape hidden rape. The American Academy of Experts in Traumatic Stress (AAETS) notes that survivors of acquaintance rape can be seen as "safe" victims, because they are much less likely to report rape or even view their nonconsensual experience as rape, precisely because they knew the perpetrator. AAETS statistics indicate that 27 percent of survivors of acquaintance rape do not consider the assault to be rape even though it meets the legal definition for rape. They also report that a full 84 percent of perpetrators of acquaintance rape insist that what they did was definitely not rape.

These statistics show why it is important to change the dialogue about rape and to highlight acquaintance rape, instead of stranger rape, as the standard for sexual violence.

Sexual Violence and Homo/Transphobia

Because rape is all about power, it can be used as a tool to oppress people who are vulnerable due to their sexual orientation or gender identity. Lesbian, gay, bi/pansexual, and transgender people can experience sexual violence and acquaintance rape just because of who they are. In these instances, rape is viewed as a punishment for not conforming to gender and sexual norms. The perpetrators of this type of sexual violence believe that raping people who do not conform to gender or sexual norms will harm or frighten those people into conforming— even though that is clearly not how gender or sexuality works. This is also called "corrective rape" or "homophobic rape" and is considered a hate crime against the LGBTQIA community. While homophobic sexual violence happens everywhere, it is most likely to occur in communities that promote inflexible gender roles, in which deviation from these norms is considered particularly shameful.

The discrimination and prejudice against gender and sexual minorities also makes it more difficult for LGBTQIA survivors to receive the medical care and support they need, and it can prevent them from feeling comfortable reporting sexual violence. The

(continued on the next page)

The LGBTQIA community celebrates Pride to honor their strength in the face of persecution and build support within the community.

(continued from the previous page)

Human Rights Campaign reports that 85 percent of advocates who work with rape survivors have counseled LGBTQIA survivors who were denied services because of their gender or sexual identity. This is particularly likely in places that use so-called "religious freedom" laws to protect people who refuse to provide services (including medical services) to people on the basis of their gender or sexual identities.

Statutory Rape

One of the requirements of consent is that all the participants must be old enough to agree to a sexual relationship. Setting these legal boundaries can be tricky when it comes to teenagers, since it's important to respect adolescents' rights to body autonomy while also protecting them from age-related power imbalances that can place unfair pressure on young teens. The actual age of consent varies from state to state, but it generally hovers around sixteen. Most states also have "Romeo and Juliet" laws, which are exceptions for sexual partners who are close in age (usually three or four years apart), assuming that the older partner is not in a position of authority over the younger.

Drug-Facilitated Rape

For your consent to be informed and freely given, it is important that your judgment is not clouded by drugs or alcohol when you give permission. It is never OK for someone to take advantage of the fact you have been drinking or using drugs. It is definitely never OK for someone to serve you alcohol or drugs for the purpose of lowering your inhibitions or rendering you unconscious in order to rape you.

When it comes to drug-facilitated rape, people usually talk about the possibility of being "roofied"—having someone spike your drink with alcohol or drugs without your knowledge. The most common substances used for this purpose are Rohypnol, GHB, ketamine, and alcohol.

The term "roofied" derives from the use of the sedative Rohypnol to facilitate sexual assault. This drug is usually a white tablet that dissolves in liquid, leaving no noticeable change in appearance, smell, or taste. The most common responses to ingesting Rohypnol are muscle relaxation, feeling drowsy or having trouble staying awake, dizziness, confusion, and difficulty remembering what happened.

Serving alcohol to lower someone's inhibitions or taking advantage of someone who has been drinking are forms of sexual violence.

GHB, or liquid ecstasy, is another common substance used to spike drinks. This powder also dissolves in liquids but leaves a slight salty taste. At low doses, GHB will make you feel drowsy and nauseated and distort your vision. At high doses, it can cause seizures, difficulty breathing, vomiting, loss of consciousness, and even coma.

Ketamine, or Special K, is a veterinary drug that usually comes as a tasteless, odorless liquid. Its effects are sedative and dissociative, which means that you might experience sights and sounds in a distorted manner and feel detached from your body. Ketamine causes hallucinations, dizziness, trouble speaking, nausea, impaired motor function, and amnesia.

The most common substance used to facilitate rape is also the most readily available: alcohol. Consuming alcohol makes it more difficult to think clearly or accurately assess a situation for danger. It is also more difficult to say no, fight, or run away under the influence of alcohol. Even one or two drinks can begin to impact memory, and it is not uncommon to black out from alcohol consumption.

Because drinking is a normal activity in many cultures, it is easy to overlook alcohol as a drug used to facilitate rape or to minimize the act of using alcohol to engage in nonconsensual sex (rape). Any time that someone serves you alcohol to lower your inhibitions (thereby making it impossible for you to give informed consent) or takes advantage of you while you are intoxicated, it is drug-facilitated rape. You have the right to expect safety even if you are drinking or using drugs; choosing to drink or use drugs never means that rape is your fault.

Drinking Safety Precautions

Rape is never your fault, even if you have been drinking or using drugs, and even if your drinking or using is illegal. You have the right to be safe from sexual violence, regardless of circumstances, and other people have the responsibility not to rape you. It's still important to know the risks and follow a personal code to reduce your risk, especially if you are drinking or using drugs.

- Don't accept drinks from other people—even someone you know—especially if that drink is served in an open container.
- Don't drink from common beverages like flasks or punch bowls.
- Don't share drinks with anyone.
- Don't leave your drink unattended even for a short time, and pour out any drink you do leave unattended.
- If your drink tastes or smells unusual, pour it out immediately.
- Always go places with a friend you trust and keep an eye out for each other.
- If you feel drunk but haven't been drinking, or if you are drinking but you feel more intoxicated than you expected, seek help right away.

Most of all, trust your gut. If you find yourself in a situation that makes you feel uncomfortable, get yourself out of that place and somewhere safe. This is much more important than any consequences that could arise from the fact you were drinking or using drugs. If you can, identify someone you know you can trust to call any time you find yourself in a situation you think might be unsafe. Having this person in mind ahead of time might make it easier for you to listen to your instincts in the moment.

Coercive Rape

When most people think about rape, they usually imagine physical violence or brute force, but that isn't always the case. Simply put, coercion means persuading someone to do something they are unwilling to do or unsure about doing. When it comes to sex, your consent should mean that you have said yes without any pressure and without factors impairing your judgment (like alcohol or drugs).

Coercion could look like someone threatening to leave you or to tell people you are being prude if you don't have sex with him or her. It could look like someone pressuring you to have sex or refusing to

Sexual violence does not always include physical force. Pressuring people to have sex or making them feel like they can't say no is coercive rape, and it is never OK.

listen when you have said you aren't interested or ready. It could also look like someone trying to make you feel guilty if you say no—for example, because he or she bought you dinner—or getting angry if you say no. In all of these scenarios, someone is trying to manipulate you into doing something you aren't sure about doing. Coercion is the opposite of ongoing, freely given, specific, informed, and enthusiastic consent. If you say yes because you fear the consequences of saying no, that is sexual violence.

CHAPTER THREE

The Effects of Sexual Violence

One of the most difficult aspects of sexual violence is that the impact of that one event can ripple out indefinitely, continuing to affect the survivor's life for years to come. These effects can be physical or emotional and can change how survivors view themselves and their relationships with other people for a long time or even forever. This is especially true when sexual violence happens at the hands of someone you trust or even love. AAETS reports that 82 percent of survivors describe themselves as "permanently changed" after acquaintance rape.

Moving Toward Recovery: The Psychological Impact of Rape

After experiencing a trauma like sexual violence, the psychological effects of the violation can be both immediate and long lasting. According to RAINN, 94 percent of rape survivors experience symptoms of post-traumatic stress disorder (PTSD) in the first two weeks following the assault. A third of survivors continue to report PTSD symptoms nine months after the rape. This is much higher than the incidence of lingering distress associated with other crimes, and the severity and longevity of PTSD associated with sexual assault is more serious even than the PTSD reported by soldiers deployed to combat zones. "While between 10 to 20 percent of war vets develop the disorder, about 70 percent of sexual assault victims experience moderate to severe distress," according to Carrie Arnold in a 2016 article in *Women's Health* magazine.

This response is so common that some experts also call the cluster of physical, psychological, and behavioral symptoms emerging after sexual violence "post-traumatic rape syndrome" or "rape trauma syndrome." It is important to remember that these are normal human responses to abnormal experiences (trauma), and they do not indicate mental illness. If you are diagnosed with a trauma syndrome or disorder, it means that you are a healthy person responding in a natural way to unnatural circumstances.

Somatic, or physical, symptoms after trauma can include shock (feeling cold, faint, disoriented, or nauseated); headaches, pain, or soreness in the body; sleep disturbances (both exhaustion and difficulty falling or staying asleep); and eating disturbances (not eating, eating less, or eating more than usual).

Psychological symptoms can include fear, anxiety, guilt or blaming yourself, humiliation and shame, helplessness or lack of control, anger, feeling dirty, memory loss, numbness, thinking about the rape all the time or having flashbacks where it feels like the rape is happening again, nightmares, depression, and hopelessness.

Behavioral symptoms after trauma can include increased crying, concentration problems, restlessness, either avoiding social interaction or seeking more social interaction than usual to fill up your time, hypervigilance, avoiding reminders of the rape, sexual dysfunction (fear of sex, decreased interest in sex, or inability to experience sexual pleasure), difficulties in relationships or at school or work, making major life changes, and acting as if nothing happened (denial).

Post-traumatic stress disorder (PTSD) is a common response after experiencing sexual violence, and it does not mean there is something wrong with you.

In the time following date rape or acquaintance rape, some survivors feel that their sense of control over their bodies and lives has been stolen and they struggle to reassert their agency. Some ways of doing this can actually hurt the survivor. These include self-harm (cutting, burning, or otherwise hurting your own body), substance abuse, eating disorders, and even suicide.

It is important to seek support after you experience a trauma like sexual violence, especially if you find yourself struggling to cope or experiencing symptoms of PTSD.

While all survivors of rape and sexual assault benefit from the support of a professional therapist, it is especially important to seek help if you find yourself struggling with coping strategies that could hurt you, or if you suspect that you are experiencing symptoms of PTSD. Some ways to get in touch with a therapist include:

- Asking your school counselor or teacher for help.
- Talking with your doctor.
- Visiting Planned Parenthood and asking for a counseling referral.
- Calling or texting a crisis line.
- Using 2-1-1 or Aunt Bertha to connect you with local resources.

Coping with Panic and Flashbacks After Rape

Experiencing acute anxiety, panic, or flashbacks after rape can be terrifying. It might make you feel like the rape is happening all over again, or like you will never feel safe.

One thing that can help is to recognize potential "triggers," or things that might spark a panic response or flashback for you. These could be things like people, places, sights, sounds, or smells that you associate with the rape. Noticing your triggers might help you stay in the present or move through the panic more quickly. This is especially true if you can recognize a potential trigger before it happens and feel prepared rather than surprised.

It might also help to remind yourself that what you are feeling is not really happening right now. Even though you feel just as unsafe as you did before, you aren't in danger. You are responding to a past event as if it is happening in the present. You might say this in your head or out loud to make it feel true.

Another strategy for panic and flashbacks is called grounding, which is really about keeping your mind in the present moment. Some people use tapping or mindfulness exercises. A common mindfulness exercise focuses on using your five senses to strengthen your connection to your immediate surroundings right now. To perform it, take a deep breath, then look around and name out loud:

- Five things you can SEE
- Four things you can TOUCH
- Three things you can HEAR
- Two things you can SMELL
- One thing you can TASTE

A counselor or therapist can help you address lingering experiences of hyperarousal (being unable to relax or feel safe), avoidance (feeling numb about everything or changing your life to escape triggers), or intrusive thoughts (flashbacks). Moving through trauma into recovery can be a long, difficult road, and a counselor or therapist is like a guide who can support you as you do that work. Some people worry that therapy is associated with mental illness or weakness of some kind, but that is not true. Recognizing that you need help recovering from trauma is one of the healthiest, strongest choices you can make.

Common Symptoms and Feelings After Sexual Assault

Everyone responds to trauma differently, and any way you feel after sexual assault is OK. Sometimes it is comforting to know the reactions that other people have reported after sexual trauma.

Common Emotional Responses:
- Shock, feeling numb, or denial
- Feeling dirty
- Anxiety
- Worrying about your safety
- Depression
- Embarrassment or shame
- Feeling like you are not in control of your life
- Fear

(continued on the next page)

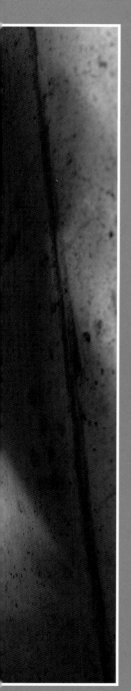

(continued from the previous page)

- Inability to trust
- Anger or irritability
- Difficulty making decisions or feeling stuck
- Seeing the world differently than you used to
- Crying or being unable to cry

Common Physical Responses:
- Fatigue or changes in sleeping or eating
- Flashbacks and nightmares
- Muscle tension or shaking
- Pain
- Shortness of breath
- Gynecological disturbances or sexual dysfunction

You may experience a combination of these responses, or you may experience something completely different.

There is no "right" way to feel after experiencing sexual violence. Different people respond to trauma in different ways. Some people may feel numb.

The Emotional Price of Violence by Someone You Trust

Date rape or acquaintance rape can be doubly painful because, in addition to the trauma associated with the sexual assault, you may also struggle with grief, shame, and self-doubt precisely because it happened at the hands of someone you know and trusted. Because you know the person who raped you in another context and have a history with him or her, you may question yourself and your perceptions. This is especially true if the people you tell about the rape seem surprised or even doubtful. You may blame yourself for allowing this person in your life in the first place and question all your instincts, since this danger flew right under your radar. And you may struggle to trust other people after having your trust broken so profoundly.

All these feelings are normal reactions to date rape or acquaintance rape. You are not responsible for anyone else's actions, and you certainly can't be expected to read someone's mind or know what is in his or her heart. The most important thing to remember is that it was not your fault, and there is nothing you could have done to anticipate or prevent it. No matter how you feel, you can trust that your emotions are normal and that you are handling them the best way you can.

The Physical Impact of Rape

The physical impact of acquaintance rape can feel overwhelming. In addition to the emotional and psychological pain associated with sexual violence, survivors must contend with the very real possibilities of physical injury, sexually transmitted infections (STIs), and pregnancy.

When it comes to physical injury, some common experiences include: bruises, cuts, or other signs of physical force; urinary tract infection; and vaginal or anal injury or bleeding. In the case of date or acquaintance rape, you can still experience physical symptoms even without physical force. In the case of drug-facilitated rape, you may experience lingering effects from the substance used to intoxicate you. If you suspect this, it is important to seek medical help since some substances can impact your body in ways you can't see.

Another significant concern may be the potential of contracting an STI—also sometimes called a sexually transmitted disease (STD) or venereal disease (VD). Some STIs require treatment to ease symptoms (although many people with STIs don't experience symptoms at all) or prevent secondary infection that could damage your reproductive system. STI screening and prophylaxis are reasons it is important to seek medical care after sexual violence. Prophylaxis means that you can receive treatment to prevent some of the most common STIs that can occur after rape. These include chlamydia, gonorrhea, trichomoniasis, bacterial vaginosis, and hepatitis B. It is also possible to treat human immunodeficiency virus (HIV, the virus that causes AIDS) prophylactically (called PEP for post-exposure prophylaxis) within the first seventy-two hours after exposure. Some STIs like hepatitis C and herpes can't be treated this way.

It can be scary to face the possibility of exposure to an STI, especially because some STIs are cannot be cured, but it is important to get screened and, if necessary, receive medical treatment for the infection. Some people feel embarrassed or ashamed about their STI status, but people who have STIs lead full and happy lives, including having healthy sex lives and starting families. Even though it might feel overwhelming, having an STI is not different from any other health concern that may come up for you over the course of your life.

Another potentially life-altering physical consequence of rape is pregnancy. According to RAINN, the chances of becoming pregnant after one rape are between 3 and 5 percent. Of course, the probability is much lower if you are already using birth control or if the perpetrator used a condom. One important option is emergency contraception. If you seek medical care after rape, you may be able

A medical professional can help you assess your risk for pregnancy and give you options for preventing pregnancy after experiencing rape.

to take a pill that will prevent pregnancy. Emergency contraception is most effective if you take it within seventy-two hours of rape (sooner is better; it is at peak effectiveness within twelve hours) although it is possible it could work up to 120 hours after rape.

49

If you do become pregnant, you face big choices, including terminating the pregnancy (abortion), becoming a parent, or finding an adoptive family for the baby. You are the only person who can decide what is right for you and your life. If you become pregnant after rape and decide to become a parent or pursue adoption, it is important to know that some states extend parental rights to rapists. Planned Parenthood is a good place to get unbiased information to help you make a decision.

CHAPTER FOUR

Understanding Rape Culture

It can be difficult to understand why sexual violence happens at all, especially sexual violence committed by an acquaintance. Sexual violence does not exist in a vacuum; it is shaped by (and shapes) the culture. It is easy to view individual experiences of rape as separate, unrelated crimes, but when you view them as pieces of a whole picture, you can begin to see that social norms and attitudes poison how people view gender and sexuality. In this environment, sexual violence thrives.

What Is Rape Culture?

When researchers and activists talk about rape culture, they are describing an environment in which rape and sexual assault become normalized, or viewed as a natural or expected part of life. In rape culture, rigid beliefs about gender roles reduce fluid concepts like sex, gender, and sexuality to a simple binary (two-part) system—that is, men and women. This means drawing strict boundaries around what it means to be masculine or feminine and punishing tendencies or behaviors that violate those rules. Because of cultural misogyny (hatred of women), rape culture also elevates one sex (men) as more valuable than the other and erases all other gender identities that don't fit this binary. Under these conditions, women and girls in heterosexual relationships have less power than their male partners, and they can be viewed as objects or property.

This is not surprising considering the history associated with misogyny and sexual violence. Girls and women used to be considered the property of their fathers or husbands, and any sexual violence committed against them was treated as property damage—much like a broken window or graffiti. The punishment for those crimes sometimes included requiring the rapist to marry the victim—essentially buying her from

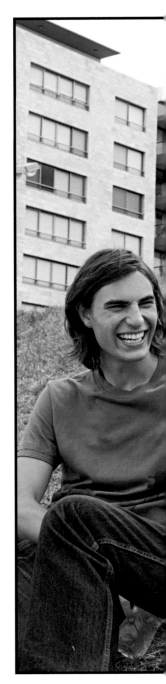

Laughing at rape jokes and talking about women as objects are both part of rape culture. This kind of toxic masculinity is harmful to everyone.

53

her father to correct the perceived crime against him. This extreme devaluing of girls and women continues in some places around the world and even in some subcultures that exist in the United States.

Most aspects of rape culture are subtler. Some common examples of rape culture include:

- Trivializing rape—making jokes about sexual violence, excusing behavior as "boys will be boys," joking about using alcohol to make a date pliable.
- Objectifying girls and women or treating them like their only worth is their bodies or how they can be useful to boys or men.
- Tolerating sexual harassment—laughing at jokes that demean women, catcalling, making sexist jokes or statements.
- Exaggerating false rape report statistics.
- Scrutinizing victims' clothing or histories (slut shaming and victim blaming).

Rape culture is a component of the heteropatriarchy. This is a system in which heterosexual, cisgender men hold the majority of the power in society. This system obviously harms girls, women, and people who are LGBTQIA, but it is also destructive to boys and men. In this environment, the qualities associated with masculinity and femininity are exaggerated, giving rise to what researchers call toxic masculinity. This is an attitude that prizes the extreme versions of so-called masculine characteristics: violence, sexual aggression, competitiveness, and lack of emotion.

Under toxic masculinity, men and boys who do not embody those attributes are degraded (usually as feminine or gay, since these things are seen as weak) and pressured to take on toxic traits to avoid being humiliated. The features of acquaintance rape—ignoring consent, entitlement to sex, viewing sex as a competition or conquest, dehumanizing women or treating them like disposable objects—all arise directly from toxic masculinity.

Another product of rape culture is the way people, including experts, talk about sexual violence and rape prevention. Many rape prevention campaigns put the responsibility for avoiding rape on the survivors or potential victims, rather than on the people who are perpetrating sexual violence. In this way, they make rape a "women's problem" and promote the idea that people who are careful can avoid being raped. This is not true, and it causes people who do experience sexual violence to blame themselves for not being careful enough. It is unfair and unreasonable for anyone to blame survivors or to expect women and other sexual minorities to live smaller, fear-driven lives, while the people with more power (usually heterosexual, cisgender men) enjoy greater freedom.

The Myth of False Accusations

Some of the reasons that survivors find it difficult to report sexual violence is because they fear they won't be believed and that they may face shaming as a result of their report. It is true that many survivors face barriers to justice, including slut

False accusations of rape are extremely rare. Survivors of sexual violence face pressure and stigma for coming forward and should always be believed.

shaming, victim blaming, and the unfair burden of having to prove their case. This is because of a cultural belief that rape statistics are exaggerated and that survivors (specifically female survivors) use false allegations of rape to undermine the lives of men. According to this cultural view, rape is an uncommon crime, and men are the real victims.

This is not true. RAINN reports that sexual violence has a false reporting rate of 2 percent, which is exactly the same as the false reporting rate for all crimes. It is extremely uncommon for someone to report sexual violence that did not happen—just like it is extremely uncommon for someone to report murders or burglaries that did not happen. The idea that rape is often falsely reported is a myth that silences survivors. Reporting sexual violence, especially acquaintance rape, is a difficult and brave task and not something people do lightly.

A more subtle form of this myth is the idea that survivors exaggerate what happened to them or change their minds after having consensual sex and decide to falsely claim they were raped. Some people who perpetuate the myth of false accusation don't even consider drug-facilitated rape or statutory rape "real" sexual violence and make excuses for these crimes, as well. This is rape culture at work.

Rape and Intersectionality

It is important to consider the intersectional nature of sexual violence. Intersectionality is the way a person's identities affect their experience of discrimination and disadvantage. For instance, a white cisgender lesbian will experience disadvantage based on her sex (female) and also based on her sexual orientation (lesbian). That same person still experiences privilege based on her race (white) and gender identity (cisgender).

When it comes to sexual violence, people whose identities are more marginalized are at greater risk. People with disabilities, LGBTQIA individuals, people of color (especially indigenous women), undocumented immigrants, and sex workers all face greater risk of experiencing sexual violence and increased barriers to accessing medical care and receiving justice. For example, undocumented immigrants may be unable to access support in their primary language and may fear loss of employment (especially if the perpetrator was an employer or coworker) and even detainment or deportation just for seeking medical care or support.

Indigenous women are twice as likely to experience sexual violence as other groups. The shameful history of genocide committed by white people against indigenous communities certainly also included sexual violence. Even stories passed down from that time (for instance, the tale of Pocahontas) diminish the sexual violence endemic in past oppression. This oppression is not just a part of history. Tribal lands retain some degree of legal sovereignty, including a separate system for prosecuting crimes. However, people who are non-Native who rape or sexually assault indigenous people on tribal land are prohibited from being tried under this system. These crimes are only subject to federal prosecution, and the federal government almost always declines those cases. This means that non-Native people can rape indigenous acquaintances or partners on tribal land without repercussion, leading some perpetrators to carefully plan their acts of sexual violence or even travel to tribal land to rape.

Trauma may be compounded in cases where people experience sexual violence that violates their specific identities. For instance, a transmasculine person who experiences vaginal rape is likely to feel the trauma associated with the sexual violence as well as trauma associated with being misgendered. Similarly, if a person feels like an outsider in the community before he is raped, this experience might exacerbate the feelings of otherness. For example, if that same transmasculine survivor already felt like an outsider in a conservative community, he might feel even more marginalized after experiencing sexual trauma— especially if the perpetrator is more accepted in the community than he is. Survivors from communities

Sometimes stories and myths attempt to romanticize real episodes of sexual violence as a way to reimagine a shameful part of history, such as in the movie *Pocahontas*.

with misogynistic views of sexual violence or that punish survivors face some of the steepest barriers to receiving support and justice. It is a good idea to seek professional support from someone who understands trauma and can also affirm your identities.

Rape Laws and Racism

It's hard to talk honestly about sexual violence without also addressing racism. The United States has a disgraceful history when it comes to the slavery of Africans and African Americans, and that history includes sexual violence. Sexual abuse and acquaintance rape perpetrated by slave owners was a common feature of slavery. Due to the nature of slavery as an institution, all children born to slaves and fathered by slave owners were conceived by rape, including those fathered by two US presidents.

Even after the abolition of slavery, the culture of white supremacy persisted. In the time immediately following abolition, the pathological (and imaginary) fear that black men were sexual predators of white women was a common excuse for lynchings, incarcerations, and murders of black men by white people. The cultural myth of black men as sexual predators persists today. The National Registry of Exonerations reports that black men are falsely incarcerated for rape at a rate three and a half times more frequent than white men. This statistic bears out even though 57 percent of perpetrators of sexual violence are white, according to RAINN. In other words, black men are far more likely to be arrested, prosecuted, and incarcerated than white men, due to racism and a racist justice system.

Black women also face specific barriers when it comes to sexual violence. Another legacy of slavery is the racist stereotype that black women are hypersexual and always sexually available. This cultural myth makes it less likely for black women to be believed when they

People of color, especially indigenous women, are more likely to experience sexual violence and face significant barriers to receiving justice.

are raped. The Department of Justice reports that black women are at higher risk of experiencing domestic violence and rape, and are significantly less likely to report sexual violence or receive justice than white women. One major barrier to black women reporting rape is the overt and institutional racism within law enforcement, which makes it an unsafe resource for some survivors.

Sexual Assault Is More than Rape

Many people assume that rape and sexual assault are the same thing. Rape is one form of sexual assault, but the term "sexual assault" refers to a range of nonconsensual acts. Sexual assault is any sexual contact at all without consent. This includes direct acts like rape and nonpenetrative sexual touching or fondling but also subtler attacks on sexual agency, like sexual harassment and catcalling. Sexual harassment is anything sexual or obscene in nature that makes you feel uncomfortable in a professional, educational, or social environment. This includes unwanted touching, flirting, jokes, requests for sexual favors, or bullying related to sex or your gender identity. Catcalling is a component of sexual harassment and occurs when someone whistles, shouts, or calls out as you pass by.

All of these things are damaging because they demean or humiliate victims as a means of exerting dominance—even if the perpetrator does not realize his motivations. Sexual harassment is a good example of how impact (how the recipient feels about something) matters more than intent (what the perpetrator meant to do or convey). Because toxic masculinity and rape culture are so embedded in our society, sometimes people behave in inappropriate or harmful ways without even realizing what they are doing. This does not change the impact or make the harassment tolerable, but it illustrates how important it is to educate all members of society (especially boys and men) and adopt zero tolerance policies for even nonphysical sexual violence.

CHAPTER FIVE

What to Do if You Are Raped

The time immediately following sexual violence can feel intense. You might be in shock, and your body may be pumping with adrenaline. It can be difficult to think or make decisions under those circumstances. Once your immediate reaction abates, a range of other feelings can pour in. Knowing your options for responding to acquaintance rape might help you process your next steps.

It Is Not Your Fault

Nothing you read or hear about sexual violence is as important as this: no matter what happened, it is not your fault. There is nothing you can do to cause someone to rape you, and there was nothing you could have done differently to prevent it. What happened to you is real. What happened to you matters. You are not alone, and you are strong enough to get through this.

Steps to Take After Rape

Immediately after sexual violence, you might not know what to do. It might even be hard to think. You experienced a trauma, and it makes sense that you are in shock. Every aspect of dealing with the aftermath of rape can be emotionally draining and difficult to face. Some of the steps you may be asked to take might feel overwhelming or make you uncomfortable. You may feel embarrassed. You may also feel angry because it is unfair that your life continues to be impacted while the perpetrator's is not. All of your feelings are valid. This is hard, but trust that you are strong. You have already survived sexual violence, and you will get through this part, too.

Make Sure You Are Safe

The very first thing you should do after you experience rape is take inventory of your immediate physical and emotional safety. Make sure that, wherever you are, you are not in any physical danger and you are not around any people who feel unsafe to you. If the person who raped you lives with you or is sharing space with you, find a way to go somewhere else.

It's always a good idea to talk to a supportive friend if you have experienced sexual violence. A friend can help you through the process and provide emotional support.

Tell Someone You Trust

It's a good idea to tell someone what happened to you right away. The most important reason to reach out to someone is so that you can get support, but it also gives you a powerful witness. This person might be able to help you seek justice, but more importantly, over the coming days and months it could help to have someone who has shared this history with you.

If Possible, Don't Make Any Changes to Your Appearance

One of your first impulses might be to change your clothing, take a bath or shower, use the bathroom, or brush your teeth. Even though you want to wash away what happened to you and feel clean and in control, it is important to preserve your appearance, especially if you decide to have a sexual assault exam. Any injuries or evidence, including bodily fluids that may be on your skin or inside

69

If you aren't sure where to go for medical care after experiencing sexual violence, advocates from Planned Parenthood or the National Sexual Assault Hotline can help you.

your mouth, vagina, or anus, can be important. You should also try to avoid eating, drinking, or smoking.

Seek Medical Care

It is important to visit a doctor or medical clinic as soon as you can after you experience rape. Some of the treatment options available to prevent contracting an STI or becoming pregnant are time sensitive. Ideally, you should visit a medical care provider immediately, but if you can't do that, it is best to be seen within seventy-two hours. Depending on the time of day or night, you can always visit your primary care physician, an urgent care or reproductive clinic, or even the emergency room. If you aren't sure where to go in your area, you can get a specific local referral from Planned Parenthood or by calling the 24/7 National Sexual Assault Hotline at (800) 656-HOPE.

Sometimes a referring organization can also connect you with a local advocate or support person who can accompany you. If not, it's a good idea to take a friend or relative so that you aren't alone. Other things you will want to bring with you include: your driver's license or other identification, your insurance card (if you have one), your phone, a hoodie or jacket (it can be cold), and a change of clothes, since the clinic staff might keep your clothing as part of a rape kit.

What Happens During a Sexual Assault Exam?

You have the option to undergo a forensic medical exam to collect evidence for a rape kit, which may be used to prosecute the perpetrator. Either a doctor or a specifically trained nurse called a sexual assault nurse examiner (SANE) will perform this exam. It's important to remember that a sexual assault exam

A sexual assault nurse examiner is trained to identify injuries and collect evidence that may help if you decide to prosecute the perpetrator.

requires your consent; you can say no to any part of the exam at any time for any reason.

Forensic exams take a long time—usually around three hours. The examiner will ask very specific questions about what happened during the rape and about your bodily functions, including details about your menstrual cycle, if you have one, and the things you have done in the time between the rape and the exam. It's OK if you can't remember all the details; it's normal to struggle with memory after trauma.

The examiner will examine your body carefully, probably using a light, for bruises, abrasions, or tender areas. If she finds anything, she will take photos. She will also do this for your genital area, examining internally and externally for signs of injury or any evidence that might remain on or inside your body. If you have a vagina, part of the exam will be a lot like a pelvic exam; if you don't feel comfortable with a speculum, you can say no.

The examiner will swab any part of your body that might have retained the perpetrator's body fluids, including your genitals (both inside and outside), your mouth, your anus, and your chest. If you have pubic hair, she might comb it for evidence. She may take clippings of your fingernails as well as hair, blood, and urine samples. The clothing you are wearing will probably be sent with your rape kit.

Get Support for Your Recovery

What you experienced is a trauma, and it may take a long time to feel like you are OK again. Some people feel very private about the sexual violence they experienced, but if you can reach out to someone, that support can make a big difference. You can talk with friends or family, a therapist or school counselor, a counselor from a local crisis center, or even a representative from a national support line. If you call or text a support line, you can remain anonymous and talk with the counselor who answers your call or text about anything at all. That person will help you talk through your immediate feelings and might even be able to offer you resources you can use later. Unless you are in imminent danger of suicide, no one will ever know you contacted a crisis line.

Reporting Rape

Reporting sexual violence can feel intimidating. You can expect that the person who takes your report will be specifically trained to work with survivors and may be part of a task force (Sexual Assault Response Team, or SART) geared toward making the process as easy as possible for you. Once reported, the crime can be investigated, and the perpetrator might be held accountable. It's important to remember that

In 2014, the White House Task Force to Protect Students from Sexual Assault launched the "It's On Us" campaign to raise awareness and end sexual assault.

acquaintance rape is just as reportable as stranger rape. It doesn't matter if you have a romantic relationship with the perpetrator or have had sex with that person before. It doesn't matter if you were drinking or using drugs (even if those things are illegal). You should be taken seriously and treated respectfully while reporting sexual violence.

There are many reasons that someone might choose not to report rape or sexual assault, and those reasons are also valid. It is true that reporting rape can make the survivor feel vulnerable and open to speculation and doubt. Some people are afraid of the possible repercussions of reporting sexual violence, especially if the perpetrator plays a significant role in their life or has been abusive or threatening. And some people have valid reasons not to trust law enforcement to treat them fairly. Sometimes people pressure survivors to report sexual violence by saying that they will be responsible if the perpetrator harms another person. This is not true. The only person responsible for sexual violence is the perpetrator. Survivors should not be pressured to do anything that makes them uncomfortable or afraid, including filing a report.

However, the situation is more complicated if the survivor is a minor. People who are mandated reporters (for example, doctors, teachers, counselors, and even all adults in some states) are required by law to report any abuse or sexual violence involving a minor that is disclosed to them. While these laws serve to keep children and teens safe, it can be difficult for young survivors, who may feel this is one more choice they aren't making themselves.

10 Great Questions to Ask a Therapist or Counselor

1. What license do you have, and how long have you been working as a therapist?

2. Do you have experience with _____? (sexual violence, acquaintance rape, trauma, PTSD symptoms, etc.)

3. I am here because _____. How do you usually approach this in therapy?

4. Do you accept my insurance?

5. What happens if I miss a session or am late for a session?

6. Are you familiar with my perspective as a _____? (community or identity)

7. Is your approach religious or informed by a specific religion?

8. Will there be homework between sessions?

9. Would anyone (family, law enforcement, etc.) have to know the topics we cover in counseling?

10. What are your strengths as a therapist?

CHAPTER SIX

Responding to Sexual Violence and Rape Culture

Thinking about sexual violence can be overwhelming and it may even make you feel like a target. There is reason to be hopeful, though. The overall rate of rape and sexual assault fell by 63 percent between 1993 and 2014, according to RAINN, which means that societal changes can impact sexual violence. Calls for survivors to share their stories as part of the #MeToo movement suggest that even greater progress could be on the horizon.

While the #MeToo initiative went viral in 2017, inspiring celebrities and noncelebrities alike to speak out about sexual assault and harassment, the idea preceded even the advent of hashtags. In 2006, civil rights activist Tarana Burke coined "Me

Too" as a component of her nonprofit organization Just Be Inc., which focuses on supporting the well-being of young women of color. A little over a decade later, millions of people used #MeToo to speak openly about sexual violence and begin to alter the national discourse on the issue.

It's important to remember that rape culture is not natural; it is a product of social norms. As people like you dismantle the false and harmful beliefs holding up rape culture, it will become increasingly less powerful and perhaps eventually become another shameful artifact of history.

Empower Your Response

You are never responsible for the sexual violence you experience, and the responsibility for preventing rape lies squarely on the shoulders of perpetrators and potential perpetrators. That does not mean you are defenseless. When it comes to empowering your response to rape culture, evidence suggests that your best tool is simple: knowing and trusting yourself.

Know What You Want

This guideline is really aimed at reducing your risk of partner rape, including coercion. If you know what you want your sexual relationships to look like and what sexual activities you want or don't want to engage in, you can be more aware of how a partner may be pressuring you or ignoring your consent.

Practice Speaking Up

One outgrowth of rigid gender roles and gender-based stereotyping is that girls and women can feel pressure to appear demure or unassertive. When you have been trained this way, it can be difficult to find your voice and use it. Assertiveness is not a masculine trait. (Nothing is!) It might be helpful to practice speaking up in low-pressure situations to build your confidence.

Pay Attention

Being aware of who is around you and what is going on near you is a good way to recognize danger before it becomes imminent. When you actively notice details in your surroundings, you are more likely to recognize if something feels wrong. This does not mean that you need to walk through life in a state of hypervigilance; you can trust your gut. Paying attention also refers to the messaging that you receive about sexual violence, gender, and sexuality from the

It's important to be aware of the messages you receive about gender, sexuality, and sexual violence from the media and the world around you.

media and from traditional authorities. For example, does your school have a dress code that dictates the length of girls' skirts or shorts? Consider the message this dress code is sending to students: that girls are responsible for other people's reactions to their bodies and that it's their fault if other people are distracted by their bodies. These kinds of subtly toxic messages can impact how you view yourself and the world around you. Being a thoughtful consumer of messaging puts you in control.

Be Thoughtful in Your Use of Alcohol and Drugs

It is never your fault if you experience sexual violence while you are drinking or using drugs, even if those things are against the law. You have the right to be safe no matter what you are doing or consuming. Still, making intentional decisions about your alcohol or drug use is a powerful choice. Some good guidelines include only drinking or using drugs in environments you know to be safe, limiting your consumption so that you remain able to think clearly, only drinking or using drugs whose source you know, and taking turns being the designated sober friend.

Listen to What People Tell You About Themselves

Writer and civil rights activist Maya Angelou said this best: "When someone shows you who they are, believe

Maya Angelou (1928–2014) was a poet, author, and civil rights activist who believed that people reveal their character through

them the first time." You can tell a great deal from spending time with someone and watching how they interact with other people. Some signs that a person is unsafe include telling degrading jokes (including rape jokes) or laughing at them, any history of violent behavior, displaying misogynistic tendencies or espousing strict gender roles, showing signs of jealousy or possessiveness, or demonstrating an inability to accept no for an answer (in any context, sexual or not). You can't know someone's interior thoughts or feelings, but you can often recognize warning signs.

Bystander Intervention

A time might come when you find yourself witnessing something unsafe happening to someone else. People who witness a crime or dangerous event but who aren't personally involved are called bystanders, and their intervention can make a big difference in the outcome. The truth is that many perpetrators or potential perpetrators are influenced by the people around them. Speaking up when you hear or see something wrong is a powerful choice.

The first step of bystander intervention is to assess the situation for your own safety. Just like you put on your own oxygen mask first on an airplane, you can't help someone in danger if you aren't safe yourself. If you do not feel like you can safely intervene, your best choice is to find someone who can, such as by calling emergency services at 9-1-1. Try to notice details and give the operator as much information as you can about the location and events. If you can safely do so, don't leave until a responder arrives.

In many cases, you may be able to use your instincts to notice that something feels off before it becomes too dangerous to intervene. For instance, if you see that someone seems uncomfortable or that someone is acting in a predatory manner, you might approach the potential victim and begin a conversation, such as asking for directions or talking about the weather. In some cases, the fact that this person is no longer alone will be enough to ward off the potential perpetrator. Similarly, if you witness an act of violence against another person, approaching the victim and letting her know that you witnessed it might make a big difference.

Remember: assess the situation for your own safety, and then provide support for the person who is in danger.

Be Aware of Warning Signs in Your Relationships

Similarly, pay attention to any violent, controlling, or degrading tendencies, no matter how minor, in your romantic relationships. Do not stay in a relationship with someone who gives off warning signs, even if those warning signs are intermittent or coupled with good qualities.

Stay Connected with Other People

It's true that there is safety in numbers. Choosing to go places with friends and letting people know your plans ahead of time both increase your personal safety. Many abusers or perpetrators of sexual violence attempt to isolate people they want to victimize. Having and maintaining a solid support system can make it more difficult for anyone to harm you.

Trust Your Instincts

This is the bottom line when it comes to keeping yourself as safe as you possibly can. If your gut tells you that there is something wrong, believe it without question. Your instincts and gut feelings are there for one reason: to keep you safe.

Choosing Healthy Relationships and Friendships

While acquaintance rape is not restricted to romantic relationships, it is important to note the link between partner rape and domestic violence. Even if your relationship is not physically violent, there are some key warning signs that can indicate an unhealthy or abusive relationship. These signs can also be a warning that your partner might disregard your sexual consent.

Some of the most common signs of unhealthy or abusive romantic relationships include: telling you what to do; causing you any sort of physical pain; an explosive temper (including acting out against pets or objects); isolating you from your friends or family; putting you down or making you feel small; accusing you of cheating; acting jealous, insecure, or possessive; checking or monitoring your phone, email, or social networks; and pressuring you to have sex.

It's possible to love someone and still recognize that that person (or your relationship) is unhealthy. Sometimes people who are very empathetic or caregiving enter relationships or continue relationships because they want to help their partner or fix them. This is a dangerous choice. If you are in a relationship where

Trust your instincts about the people around you. People with rigid beliefs and those who don't accept no for an answer are not safe or healthy to be around.

there are signs of abuse or unhealthy behaviors, it is important to tell someone about it. Talk to a friend, family member, or trusted adult (teacher, doctor, counselor) who can help you navigate the push/pull of loving someone who might be unhealthy for you.

Unhealthy and abusive relationships aren't limited to romantic ones. If you notice that people around you don't listen when someone tells them no (even in nonsexual situations) or hold rigid beliefs about sex and gender, those are red flags. If you see or hear people demean others based on immutable qualities (for example, sex, gender, sexual or gender identities, race or ethnicity) or if they trivialize sexual violence by making or enjoying rape jokes, those are all clear signs that they aren't safe. If you speak up about something and people belittle you or don't listen to you, this speaks volumes about their characters.

You deserve to be surrounded by people who love you and respect you and who have healthy worldviews. It can be painful to walk away from friends or partners who aren't safe, but it is also empowering. Developing your interests, hobbies, and worldviews, and reaching out to other people who share those things (both online and offline) are good ways to widen your social circle and make sure that you have strong, healthy connections.

Having the support of a sincere friend can make all the difference after experiencing acquaintance rape or another kind of sexual violence.

How to Support a Friend After Rape

It can be challenging to support someone who has experienced trauma. Knowing what to say (and what not to say) and do ahead of time can be helpful.

- **Believe the survivor.** This seems obvious but might be harder than it seems, especially if you know and care about the person who perpetrated the rape. Remember that even people who are likeable or who have good qualities can commit rape. Also remember that false reporting is very rare, but survivors face intense scrutiny anyway. The most important thing you can do for your friend is to believe them and not question what they tell you.

- **Do not ask questions that blame the survivor.** To ensure that you don't inadvertently send the message that you don't believe your friend, avoid asking loaded questions. Examples include: Did you flirt or lead him on? Are you sure? Were you drinking?

- **Listen without advising.** Your friend has experienced a violation that impacted her agency. It's important to honor that by listening to what she says without an agenda and without telling her how to feel or what to do.
- **Help your friend get medical care.** It's important for your friend to receive medical care, especially if she might need emergency contraception or STI prophylaxis. If your friend agrees, help her find a place to go and accompany her. Your presence can make your friend feel supported and help her remember things the medical provider said if she's in shock.
- **Support your friend's sense of safety.** It may take a long time for your friend to feel safe again. Let your friend know that you are there to help him feel safer. This might mean walking with him to class or helping him avoid places or people that are upsetting.

Ending and Preventing Sexual Violence

In some ways it seems like ending sexual violence is simple: perpetrators must stop committing sexual assault and rape. Period.

This requires addressing obvious perpetrators and overt sexual violence, but also weeding out the less conspicuous ways that society ignores (or trivializes) sexual violence and upholds stereotypes. Toxic masculinity and rigid beliefs about gender and sexuality harm everyone, even people whose gender and sexual identities are deemed acceptable. Ending sexual violence means dismantling rape culture.

One way to begin doing this is for schools and communities to actively teach about consent and sexual violence in ways that empower social change. Young people deserve to learn how consent works— and to be held accountable for behaviors that violate consent, even outside of sexual relationships. Educational initiatives and everyday influencers must specifically teach those with the most social power (usually heterosexual cisgender boys and men) what sexual assault and rape actually look like and how to prevent those acts, especially if that requires behaviors that defy cultural expectations for what it means to be masculine. This education should also include zero tolerance policies for the subtle (and not so subtle) ways that people and institutions perpetuate misogyny, homo/transphobia, and white supremacy.

Importantly, adults must take stock of the ways they dismiss consent, especially the nonsexual consent of young people. Authoritarian structures in schools and homes perpetuate the idea that being larger or stronger or older or more powerful means using that power to get your way, even against the will of someone who is smaller or weaker or younger or has less power. This is a part of rape culture.

Finally, dismantling toxic social norms requires people to acknowledge their own privilege and use it to make the world safer for everyone. Privilege means the ways in which you have more power than other people, for instance, because of your gender, race, class background, education, or sexual orientation. An important part of acknowledging privilege is recognizing when to step back, listen, and allow other people to lead. Survivors and the people most vulnerable to sexual violence should be driving the conversation about rape culture—and they should not accept the burden of responsibility for preventing it. Every survivor who speaks out about their experience shatters the silence surrounding acquaintance rape, and every person who speaks up against rape culture moves society one step closer to ending sexual violence.

agency An individual's power and ability to make a free choice.

agender Denoting a person who does not identify as having any gender.

bias A belief or behavior that shows favor toward a certain thing, person, or group of people; the opposite of a neutral viewpoint or open mind.

body autonomy Self-governing control over how you use your body.

cisgender Denoting a person whose gender identity matches the sex they were assigned at birth; not transgender.

coercion Force or fear used to control someone or persuade them to do something.

consent Permission or agreement for something to happen.

gender norms A set of social expectations defining acceptable behaviors or attitudes based on someone's perceived gender.

genderqueer Denoting a person who does not identify as either male or female.

heteropatriarchy A sociopolitical hierarchy in which most of the power is held by heterosexual, cisgender men.

homophobia Dislike or discrimination against people who are gay, lesbian, bi/pansexual, or queer.

intersectionality The ways that a person's

identities (race, sex, gender identity, sexuality, etc.) overlap and accumulate experiences of disadvantage or discrimination.

LGBTQIA Lesbian, gay, bisexual, transgender, queer, intersex, or asexual.

mindfulness Focusing on the present moment and accepting your feelings, thoughts, and physical sensations without judgment.

nonbinary Rejecting binary categories; often denoting a gender identity that is neither male nor female.

normalization The way that ideas and behaviors become accepted as natural or "normal" parts of life.

prophylaxis A treatment taken to prevent illness or disease.

rape culture The way that social attitudes make rape seem normal or trivial.

slut shaming Making a person feel guilt or shame for real or perceived sexual activity or for violating social norms for dress or behavior.

toxic masculinity Exaggerated social norms for maleness that harm people of all genders.

transgender Denoting a person whose gender identify is different from the biological sex they were assigned at birth.

transmasculine Denoting a person who was assigned female at birth but whose gender identity is male or who identifies with masculinity.

transphobia Dislike or discrimination against people who are transgender or whose gender identity or expression differs from the sex they were assigned at birth.

trauma Occurrences outside the realm of normal human experience that cause significant distress.

victim blaming Assigning all or partial responsibility for a crime or abuse to the person who experienced the crime or abuse.

For More Information

Canadian Centre for Men and Families
201-2 Homewood Avenue
Toronto, ON M4Y2J9
Canada
(647) 479-9611 or toll free at (1-844) 900-2263
Website: http://www.menandfamilies.org
Facebook, Instagram, and Twitter: @menandfamilies
This organization provides mentoring and support
    for male victims of abuse and violence, including
    therapy, peer support, and a legal clinic.

Crisis Text Line
Text 741741
Website: https://www.crisistextline.org
Facebook, Twitter, and Instagram: @CrisisTextLine
Crisis Text Line is a free, text-based support line
    staffed twenty-four hours a day by volunteer
    crisis counselors. CTL collects and shares
    anonymous survey data to enhance crisis
    response services.

Ending Violence Association of Canada
1404-510 West Hastings Street
Vancouver, BC V6B 1L8
Canada
(604) 633-2506
Website: http://endingviolencecanada.org
This nonprofit organization works to eliminate

gender-based violence, including sexual violence, intimate partner violence, and child abuse, by providing education, programs, and resources.

Love Is Respect (formerly National Teen Dating
    Abuse Online Hotline)
(866) 331-9474
Text 22522
Website: http://www.loveisrespect.org
Facebook: @LoveIsRespectPage
Instagram: @LoveIsRespectOfficial
Twitter: @LoveIsRespect
Love Is Respect is a project of the National Domestic
    Violence Hotline that provides support for young
    people experiencing violence from romantic
    partners and aims to end dating abuse.

Men Can Stop Rape
1130 6th Street NW, Suite 100
Washington, DC 20001
(202) 265-6530
Website: http://www.mencanstoprape.org
Facebook: @mcsrape
Twitter: @MenCanStopRape
Men Can Stop Rape uses a public health approach
    to teach and empower men to prevent violence,
    especially violence against women.

Planned Parenthood
(800) 230-PLAN (7526)
Website: https://www.plannedparenthood.org
Facebook and Instagram: @PlannedParenthood
Twitter: @PPFA
Planned Parenthood is the leading global nonprofit providing sexual health care and education. It has more than six hundred health centers across the country.

Project Respect
#201- 3060 Cedar Hill Road
Coast and Straits Salish Territories
Victoria, BC V8T 3J5
Canada
(250) 383-3232
Website: https://www.yesmeansyes.com
Facebook: @ProjectRespect
Twitter: @ProjRespect
Project Respect offers workshops and educational initiatives for middle and high school students.

RAINN & National Sexual Assault Hotline
(800) 656-HOPE (4673)
Website: https://www.rainn.org
Facebook: @RAINN01
Twitter and Instagram: @RAINN
RAINN is the largest US organization combating

sexual violence through education and hotlines. The organization coordinates with local sexual assault partners and the Department of Defense.

Safe Horizon
(800) 621-HOPE (4673)
Website: https://www.safehorizon.org
Facebook, Instagram, and Twitter: @SafeHorizon
Safe Horizon is a victim assistance organization offering support and advocacy for rape, domestic violence, human trafficking, stalking, child abuse, and youth homelessness.

Start by Believing & Seek Then Speak End Violence Against Women International
145 South Main Street
Colville, WI 99114
(509) 684-9800
Website: http://www.startbybelieving.org
Facebook: @EVAWinternational
Twitter: @EVAWintl
Start by Believing and Seek Then Speak are public awareness campaigns aimed at changing the narrative on sexual violence to support survivors rather than further victimizing them. The campaigns offer support for survivors looking for resources after sexual violence.

The Trevor Project
PO Box 69232
West Hollywood, CA 90069
(866) 488-7386
Website: https://www.thetrevorproject.org
Facebook: @TheTrevorProject
Twitter & Instagram: @TrevorProject
The Trevor Project is a crisis intervention nonprofit
    specifically addressing the needs of LGBTQ
    young people.

WAVAW Rape Crisis Centre
2405 Pine Street
PO Box 46851
Vancouver, BC V6J 5M4
Canada
(604) 255-6344
Website: http://www.wavaw.ca
Facebook and Twitter: @WAVAWRCC
WAVAW is a feminist organization providing
    information, referrals, and advocacy for
    survivors of sexual violence.

Bates, Laura. *Girl Up: Kick Ass, Claim Your Woman Card, and Crush Everyday Sexism.* New York, NY: Touchstone, 2017.

Byers, Ann. *Sexual Assault and Abuse (*Confronting Violence Against Women*).* New York, NY: Rosen Publishing, 2016.

Cappiello, Katie. *Slut: A Play and Guidebook for Combating Sexism and Sexual Violence.* New York, NY: The Feminist Press at CUNY, 2015.

Clark, Annie E., and Andrea L. Pino. *We Believe You: Survivors of Campus Sexual Assault Speak Out.* New York, NY: Holt Paperbacks, 2016.

Corinna, Heather. *S.E.X: The All-You-Need-to-Know Sexuality Guide to Get You Through Your Teens and Twenties.* 2nd ed. Cambridge, MA: Da Capo Lifelong Books, 2016.

Dominy, Amy Fellner. *Die for You.* New York, NY: Delacorte Press, 2016.

Harding, Kate. *Asking for It: The Alarming Rise of Rape Culture—And What We Can Do About It.* Cambridge, MA: Da Capo Lifelong Books, 2015.

Henneberg, Susan. *I Have Been Raped. Now What?* New York, NY: Rosen Publishing, 2016.

Johnston, E. K. *Exit, Pursued by a Bear.* New York, NY: Speak, 2017.

Klein, Rebecca. *Rape and Sexual Assault: Healing and Recovery.* New York, NY: Rosen Publishing, 2014.

Lindin, Emily. *Unslut: A Diary and a Memoir.* San Francisco, CA: Zest Books, 2015.

Lohmann, Raychelle Cassada, and Sheela Raja. *The Sexual Trauma Workbook for Teen Girls: A Guide to Recovery from Sexual Assault and Abuse.* Oakland, CA: Instant Help Books, 2016.

Smith, Amber. *The Way I Used to Be.* New York, NY: Margaret K. McElderry Books, 2017.

Stoian, Maria. *Take It as a Compliment.* London, UK: Singing Dragon, 2015.

Arnold, Carrie. "Life After Rape: The Sexual Assault Issue No One's Talking About." *Women's Health*, September 13, 2016. https://www.womenshealthmag.com/life/ptsd-after-rape.

Break the Cycle. "Learning About Dating Abuse: Warning Signs." Retrieved March 17, 2018. https://www.breakthecycle.org/warning-signs.

Breiding, M. J., et al. "Prevalence and Characteristics of Sexual Violence, Stalking, and Intimate Partner Violence Victimization: National Intimate Partner and Sexual Violence Survey." *Morbidity and Mortality Weekly Report*. September 5, 2014. https://www.cdc.gov/mmwr/preview/mmwrhtml/ss6308a1.htm?s_cid=ss6308a1_e#Table1.

Curtis, David G. "Perspectives on Acquaintance Rape." The American Academy of Experts in Traumatic Stress, Inc. Retrieved March 17, 2018. http://www.aaets.org/article13.htm.

Human Rights Campaign (HRC). "Sexual Assault and the LGBTQ Community." Retrieved March 17, 2018. https://www.hrc.org/resources/sexual-assault-and-the-lgbt-community.

Minnesota Coalition Against Sexual Assault. "Step by Step Medical Forensic Exam." Retrieved March 17, 2018. http://www.mncasa.org/assets/PDFs/Step%20by%20Step%20Medical%20Forensic%20Exam.pdf.

National Alliance to End Sexual Violence. "Where We Stand: Racism and Rape." Retrieved March 17, 2018. http://www.endsexualviolence.org /where_we_stand/racism-and-rape.

Office on Women's Health, US Department of Health and Human Services. "Date Rape Drugs." Retrieved March 17, 2018. http:// www.womenshealth.gov/publications/our -publications/fact-sheet/date-rape-drugs.html.

Planned Parenthood. "All About Consent." Retrieved March 17, 2018. https://www .plannedparenthood.org/learn/teens/sex/all -about-consent.

Planned Parenthood. "What Should I Do If I Or Someone I Know Is Sexually Assaulted?" Retrieved March 17, 2018. https://www .plannedparenthood.org/learn/sex-and -relationships/sexual-consent/what-should -i-do-if-i-or-someone-i-know-was-sexually -assaulted.

RAINN. "Perpetrators of Sexual Assault: Statistics." Retrieved March 17, 2018. https://www.rainn .org/statistics/perpetrators-sexual-violence.

RAINN. "Scope of the Problem: Statistics." Retrieved March 17, 2018. https://www.rainn .org/statistics/scope-problem.

RAINN. "Victims of Sexual Violence: Statistics." Retrieved March 17, 2018. https://www.rainn .org/statistics/victims-sexual-violence.

Rape Crisis Cape Town Trust. "Rape Trauma Syndrome." Retrieved March 17, 2018. https://rapecrisis.org.za/rape-trauma-syndrome.

Rizzo, Jessica. "Native American Women Are Rape Targets Because of a Legislative Loop Hole." Vice, December 16, 2015. https://www.vice.com/en_us/article/bnpb73/native-american-women-are-rape-targets-because-of-a-legislative-loophole-511.

Safe Horizon. "After Sexual Assault: A Recovery Guide for Survivors." Retrieved March 17, 2018. https://www.safehorizon.org/wp-content/uploads/2016/07/Safe-Horizon-Sexual-Assault-Guide-2011.pdf.

Vega, Tanzina. "Study: Black People More Likely to Be Wrongfully Convicted." CNN, March 7, 2017. https://www.cnn.com/2017/03/07/politics/blacks-wrongful-convictions-study/index.html.

Index

A

abusive relationships, 76, 87, 89

acquaintance rape, 5, 6, 8, 10, 14, 22–23, 25–26, 36, 40, 46–47, 51, 55, 57, 59, 61, 66, 75, 77, 87, 94

AIDS, 48

alcohol, 16, 29–31, 33, 54

American Academy of Experts in Traumatic Stress (AAETS), 25, 36

Angelou, Maya, 82–84

Aunt Bertha, 41

avoidance, 25, 38, 42, 55, 71, 91–92

B

black community, issues around sexual violence, 61–62, 64

body autonomy, 28

Burke, Tarana, 9, 78

bystander intervention, 84–85

C

catcalling, 54, 64

cisgender people, 54–55, 58, 93

civil rights, 9, 78, 82, 83

coercive rape, 33–35

consent, 15–19
   enthusiastic consent, 19
   examples, 15–16
   informed consent, 19
   ongoing consent, 18
   specific consent, 18

contraception, 48–49

counseling, 41

crisis center, 74

D

denial, 38, 43

Department of Justice, 64

drinking precautions, 32–33

drug-facilitated rape, 29–31, 47, 57

E

eating disorders, 40

effects of rape, 36–50
   common symptoms, 43–45
   emotional impact, 46
   flashbacks, 41–43
   physical impact, 47–50
   psychological impact,

36–41
emergency contraception, 48, 49, 92
emotional impact of rape, 46
enthusiastic consent, 18, 19, 35

F

false accusations, 56–57
flashbacks, 38, 41–42, 45

G

gender norms, 26–27, 51, 94
gender roles, 27, 52, 80, 84
GHB, 29–30

H

harassment, 54, 64, 65, 78
healthy relationships, 87–89
helplessness, 38
hepatitis C, 48
herpes, 48
HIV, 48
homophobia, 26–28, 93
Human Rights Campaign, 28
hypervigilance, 38, 80

I

indigenous populations, 10, 58–60, 63
informed consent, 18–19, 29, 31, 35
intersectionality, 58–61

J

jokes, 54, 64, 84, 89
Just Be Inc., 79

K

ketamine, 29, 31

L

legislation, 28, 61–64, 76
LGBTQIA people, 10–11, 27–28, 54, 58

M

marital rape, 14, 23–24
medical care, 27, 48, 58, 70–71, 92
memory, 31, 38, 73
#MeToo, 78–79
misgendering, 59
misogyny, 52, 61, 84, 93

N

National Registry of

Exonerations, 62
National Sexual Assault
   Hotline, 71

O

objectification, 54
ongoing consent, 18, 35

P

panic, 41–42
parental rights, 50
partner rape, 23–24, 79, 87
Plan B, 49
Planned Parenthood, 18,
   41, 50, 70–71
physical impact, of rape,
   47–50
post-traumatic rape
   syndrome, 37
post-traumatic stress
   disorder (PTSD), 12,
   37, 39–41
pregnancy, 47–50, 71
prophylaxis, 47–48, 92
psychological impact of
   rape, 36–41

R

racism, 61–64
rape

acquaintance, 25–26
coercive, 33–35
definition of, 12
drug-facilitated, 29–31
marital, 23–24
partner, 23–24
statistics, 8–12
statutory, 28–29
Rape, Abuse, and Incest
   National Network
   (RAINN), 8, 10, 24–25,
   37, 48, 57, 62, 78
rape culture, 51–55
bystanders, 84–85
intersectionality, 58–61
legislation, 61–64
prevention, 92–94
relationships, 87–89
responding to, 79–84
sexual assault, 64–65
supporting others,
   91–92
rape kit, 71–73
rape trauma syndrome, 37
reporting rape, 27, 57, 64,
   74–76
Rohypnol, 29
roofies, 29

S

self-harm, 40
sexual assault exam, 69, 72–73
sexual assault nurse examiner (SANE), 72
Sexual Assault Response Team (SART), 74
sexual harassment, 54, 64–65, 78
sexually transmitted disease (STD), 47
sexually transmitted infection (STI), 47–48, 71, 92
sleep, 37–38, 45
slut shaming, 20, 54, 56
Special K, 31
specific consent, 18, 35
statutory rape, 28–29, 57
steps to take after rape, 67–74
substance abuse, 40
suicide, 12, 40, 74
supporting a friend, 91–92

T

toxic masculinity, 53, 55, 65, 93
transphobia, 26–28, 93
trauma symptoms, behavioral, 38
physical, 37–38
psychological, 38
tribal land, 59
triggers, 41–42

U

United Nations, 24
urinary tract infection, 47

V

venereal disease (VD), 47
victim blaming, 54, 57

W

warning signs, 84, 86–87

Z

zero tolerance, 65

About the Author

Melissa Mayer is a writer, volunteer crisis counselor, and former classroom teacher. She loves projects that explore the liminal spaces between science, sexuality, class, and culture, and she worked as a professional science blogger for five years. Mayer lives in Portland, Oregon, with her wife, children, and an unreasonable number of animals.

Photo Credits

Cover Terry Vine/Blend Images/Getty Images; p. 5 Stokkete /Shutterstock.com; pp. 8–9, 62–63 Chelsea Guglielmino /FilmMagic/Getty Images; pp. 10–11 Alexander Image /Shutterstock.com; pp. 12–13 Pormezz/Shutterstock.com; p. 17 Laszlo66/Shutterstock.com; p. 23 Blend Images /Shutterstock.com; p. 27 Elzbieta Sekowska/Shutterstock.com; p. 30 Cdrin/Shutterstock.com; p. 34 JackF/iStock/Thinkstock; pp. 38–39 Martin Moxter/Westend61/Getty Images; p. 40 Rob Marmion/Shutterstock.com; pp. 44–45 Lopolo /Shutterstock.com; p. 49 Justin Sullivan/Getty Images; pp. 52–53 Image Source/DigitalVision/Getty Images; p. 56, 70 Wavebreakmedia/Shutterstock.com; pp. 60–61 MARKA /Alamy Stock Photo; pp. 68–69 Syda Productions/Shutterstock.com; p. 72 Yupa Watchanakit/Shutterstock.com; p. 75 Tim Clayton /Corbis Sport/Getty Images; pp. 80–81 United Archives GmbH /Alamy Stock Photo; p. 83 Stephen Chernin/Getty Images; p. 88 Kay Blaschke/Stock4B/Getty Images; pp. 90–91 Martin-dm /E+/Getty Images.

Design and Layout: Nicole Russo-Duca; Editor: Rachel Aimee; Photo Researcher: Sherri Jackson